GETTING NEAR TO BABY

By
Y YORK

Based on the book
by
AUDREY COULOUMBIS

Dramatic Publishing
Woodstock, Illinois • Australia • New Zealand • South Africa

*** NOTICE ***

ISBN: 978-1-58342-720-0

For Audrey,
and in memory of Akila

IMPORTANT BILLING AND CREDIT REQUIREMENTS

All producers of the play must give credit to Audrey Couloumbis as the author of the book and Y York as the dramatizer of the play in all programs distributed in connection with performances of the play and in all instances in which the title of the play appears for purposes of advertising, publicizing or otherwise exploiting the play and/or a production. The names of Audrey Couloumbis and Y York must also appear on a separate line, on which no other name appears, immediately following the title, and must appear in size of type not less than fifty percent (50%) the size of the title type. Biographical information on Audrey Couloumbis and Y York, if included in the playbook, may be used in all programs. *In all programs this notice must appear:*

"Produced by special arrangement with
THE DRAMATIC PUBLISHING COMPANY of Woodstock, Illinois"

In addition, all producers of the play must include the following acknowledgment on the title page of all programs distributed in connection with performances of the play and on all advertising and promotional materials:

"*Getting Near to Baby* was first produced on March 27, 2008, at People's Light & Theatre, Malvern, Pa. Abigail Adams, Artistic Director and Grace E. Grillet, Managing Director."

Getting Near to Baby was premiered by People's Light & Theatre Company, Malvern, Pa., March 27, 2008, Abigail Adams, artistic director; Grace Grillet, managing director.

Willa Jo . . . . Claire Inie-Richards
Little Sister . . . . Maggie Fitzgerald
Aunt Polly . . . . Mary Elizabeth Scallen
Uncle Hob . . . . Christopher Patrick Mullen
Liz Fingers . . . . Katie Johantgen
Isaac Fingers . . . . Nathaniel Brastow
Lucy Wainwright . . . . Susan McKey
Cynthia Wainwright . . . . Meg Rose

Directed by. . . . . Abigail Adams
Set Designer. . . . . Jim Kronzer
Costume Designer . . . . Marla Jurglanis
Lighting Designer. Dennis Parichy
Sound Designer/Composer . . . . Christopher Colucci
Stage Manager . . . . Kate McSorley

GETTING NEAR TO BABY

CHARACTERS:

WILLA JO 12
LITTLE SISTER. 7
LIZ FINGERS. 13
ISAAC FINGERS 7
CYNTHIA WAINWRIGHT. 12
AUNT PATTY
UNCLE HOB
LUCY WAINWRIGHT

PLACE AND TIME:

In a backyard, a cave and on a roof in a small town in North Carolina in 1967.

PLAYWRIGHT'S NOTE:

LITTLE SISTER does not speak, but she hears and reacts.

ACT ONE

PROLOGUE

(Night. WILLA JO and LITTLE SISTER stand on the roof of a small house. They are wearing T-shirts and shorts. LITTLE SISTER holds a rolled-up painting.)

WILLA JO. Careful now, don't fall… Look at them stars. Look at all that sky, Little Sister. I told you I'd find us some *sky*. Is that enough sky for you?

(LITTLE SISTER raises her arms toward the heavens in an embrace.)

SCENE 1

(An uncluttered backyard and porch of a simple but clean house floating in a blue sea of a sky. There are seven large decorative yard gnomes. PATTY enters from the street with suitcases and shopping bags.)

PATTY. Come on, girls, don't dawdle. Hob! Hob, we're home.

(HOB enters.)

HOB. I kinda thought you'd be home three hours ago.

PATTY. I had to feed them—then we stopped at May's. You can't believe their clothes— *(To off.)* Willa Jo, don't let her go in the ditch— *(She snaps her shorts in a gesture of frustration.)* I'm going to have half a heart attack before this is over. Oh, Hob, you can't even imagine it. Noreen's gotten worse even than she was.

HOB. You didn't bring her?

PATTY. …I didn't even think of that. All I could think of was getting the girls away. Truth be told, they were glad to leave.

HOB. What's Noreen going to do all by herself?

PATTY. She's going to get better is what she's going to do— Hush now.

(WILLA JO and LITTLE SISTER enter; they are wearing clean but tattered dresses. LITTLE SISTER clutches the painting. Her shoes have gotten muddy.)

PATTY. Oh, Little Sister, look at your shoes!

WILLA JO. Why do you have a ditch?

PATTY. We got new neighbors. One of them's loopy as a bedbug—

HOB. Patty—

PATTY *(over)*. Larry Fingers dug that ditch in the middle of the night. Says he's going to fill it back up as soon as the weather's right, whatever that means. I bet you end up doing it, Hob.

HOB. It's not that bad.

PATTY. Say hi to your Uncle Hob.

WILLA JO. Hi, Uncle Hob.

HOB. Willa Jo. Hey, Little Sister. You musta grown a foot. *(Brief awkward pause.)*

WILLA JO. We saw you two weeks ago. She couldn'ta grown a foot since then.

PATTY. …You girls go on in— Put on your new little outfits. *(Hands them the shopping bags.)* Give me that picture, Little Sister—I'll take care of it—

(LITTLE SISTER clutches the painting.)

PATTY. Okay, then, how's about I get a frame for it? Won't that be nice?

(LITTLE SISTER does not reply.)

PATTY. Go inside and put on your new sandals. Your sneakers are filthy.

(The girls head for the porch.)

PATTY. Hey—hey. What do you think you're doing?

WILLA JO. We're going in the house like you said to.

PATTY. Go 'round through the garage.

HOB. New carpet. Your aunt's trying to keep it nice.

PATTY. You can't keep a carpet nice when you got children traipsing in and out all day long.

WILLA JO. We won't traipse. Neither one of us will traipse, will we, Little Sister?

(LITTLE SISTER touches the gnomes as she passes.)

PATTY. Careful there with my garden gnomes.

WILLA JO. She don't mean no harm. *(To LITTLE SISTER.)* Come on, I'll help you take off your shoes.

(WILLA JO and LITTLE SISTER exit.)

HOB *(brief pause)*. Wow…

PATTY. Yeah. Not a word out of her.

HOB. Why didn't you bring Noreen, Patty?

PATTY. She'd hate living with me. It would never occur to her to put something back where it belongs, and I'd just be at her every single second—she'd never get well… Oh, Hob, did I do wrong?

HOB. Don't worry. We can always go back and get her if we need to. Has she heard from Joe?

PATTY. Not a word. And she makes all these excuses to the girls—"Oh, your father loves you, he just can't call because he's working so hard." The girls *know*. They're children, but they are not stupid.

HOB. She's doing her best.

PATTY. It was awful. If I hadn't gone back the welfare would have taken the girls away. They hadn't bathed since the funeral—dishes piled up—when they need a plate they use a dirty one. How can people live like that?

HOB. They're suffering in their grief, that's how.

PATTY. You can wash a dish no matter how sad you are. By the time I left, she wouldn't even look at me. All she does is paint. And not for the greeting card company, just enormous pictures she won't let anybody see—Little Sister won't let me see it either. Noreen's going to lose her job she don't shape up.

HOB. Did you tell her to call us if she needs money?
PATTY. She knows that.
HOB. Still, it's nice to hear it.

(WILLA JO and LITTLE SISTER enter from the garage; LITTLE SISTER with the painting.)

PATTY. Well, isn't that better? A sight more comfortable than those dresses. Don't they look as cute as buttons, Hob?
HOB. Well. They look familiar.
PATTY. Of course they look familiar. They're kin.
WILLA JO. I think Uncle Hob means we're dressed like you.
PATTY. Don't sass.
WILLA JO. I didn't mean to—

(LITTLE SISTER has been poking a finger into her shoes.)

PATTY. Little Sister, quit picking at your new shoes.
WILLA JO. They hurt.
PATTY. How do you know that? Did she say something?
WILLA JO. No, ma'am. She didn't say something. I know it because mine hurt.
PATTY. They do not hurt. They're very expensive. What did you do with your dirty clothes?
WILLA JO. We left them in the bathroom.
PATTY. Did you put them in the hamper?
WILLA JO. I didn't know to.

PATTY. Well, of course that's what you do with clothes when you take them off. I'll do it. I'm going to wash all your things anyway.

WILLA JO. They're not dirty.

PATTY. They're dusty. Then we'll repack everything and put the suitcases in the attic, and when the fall comes we'll open them up, and it'll be like Christmas.

WILLA JO *(small panic)*. Christmas? We won't still be here at Christmas?

PATTY. Well, of course you won't. I'm just saying… Little Sister, you want to give me that picture now?

(LITTLE SISTER clutches the painting.)

PATTY. Right. *(Heading in.)* Hob?

HOB. I'll be right there. *(PATTY exits.)* Did you see how I fixed up your room?

WILLA JO. It looks real nice.

(LITTLE SISTER reaches into her pocket and shows a piece of candy.)

HOB. Well, now, we don't have to let your aunt see that—I don't think I remembered to get her a piece is why. Just keep it in your pocket. And be sure to brush your teeth after you eat it.

WILLA JO. Thanks for the chocolate, Uncle Hob.

HOB. You're welcome, I'm sure. I'm going to go help your aunt. *(He exits into the garage taking the rest of the suitcases.)*

WILLA JO *(fiercely)*. Let me see the picture.

(LITTLE SISTER hugs it closer.)

WILLA JO. Did Mom say you could take it? *(No reply.)* Which one is it?

(LITTLE SISTER looks up at the sky.)

WILLA JO. What are you looking at—? I don't see anything... Are you ever going to talk?... Listen to me, it wasn't your fault—it wasn't my fault—it wasn't anybody's fault—

(LITTLE SISTER walks away. WILLA JO takes the candy from her pocket. Begins to unwrap it in a solemn ritual.)

WILLA JO. Do this.

(LITTLE SISTER mimics WILLA JO's actions. They unfold and flatten the paper, place the candy on the paper on the ground.)

WILLA JO. I'm going to eat this chocolate, and when it dissolves into my mouth juices, I am going to remember something wonderful.

(WILLA JO puts the candy in her mouth; LITTLE SISTER does, too.)

WILLA JO. Mmmm. I'm remembering something wonderful. Are you remembering something wonderful?

(LITTLE SISTER nods.)

WILLA JO. You gonna tell me?

(LITTLE SISTER looks away.)

WILLA JO. …I'm remembering catching lightning bugs in a jar. I'm remembering opening the lid and lightning bugs flying away into the night.

(LITTLE SISTER counts on her fingers to eight.)

WILLA JO. That's right! There were eight bugs in that jar. I caught eight lightning bugs.

(Indignant, LITTLE SISTER gestures that she caught them.)

WILLA JO. I don't think you caught them. I think I caught them.

(LITTLE SISTER stamps her foot fiercely. WILLA JO laughs.)

WILLA JO. All right, all right—you caught them.

(LIZ and ISAAC enter and stop at the edge of the yard.)

LIZ. I'm Liz Fingers. I live across the street.

ISAAC. I'm Isaac Fingers. I live across the street. I'm seven. We saw you playing in the ditch. Look, Liz, yard fairies. *(He speaks to the gnomes.)* Hi, hi there, how you doing? What's your name?

WILLA JO. I don't know his name— *(Pointedly.)* He belongs to my Aunt Patty.

LIZ *(catching WILLA JO's meaning)*. Leave it be, Isaac.

WILLA JO. I'm Willa Jo, and this is Little Sister. We're visiting my aunt and uncle for a while.

(LITTLE SISTER holds up seven fingers. A very slight pause as LIZ realizes the little girl isn't going to speak.)

WILLA JO. She's seven, too.

ISAAC *(holds up seven fingers)*. Together we are fourteen. Fourteen fingers, Liz!

LIZ. Yep, just like how many in the Fingerses family household if you count all the uncles.

WILLA JO. There's fourteen of you?

ISAAC. In the house across the street. *(To LITTLE SISTER.)* Do you want to see my cave?

(LITTLE SISTER nods.)

ISAAC *(to LIZ)*. Can we?

LIZ. Okay, but be sure to take the flashlight.

WILLA JO. Wait—I mean—where is it?

LIZ. In the little rise behind our house. The entrance is all shored up with timbers.

ISAAC. It's irresistible.

WILLA JO. Is it safe?

LIZ. It's perfectly safe. My Uncle Larry made it.

WILLA JO. Is he the same person dug the ditch?

LIZ. Yes, but he didn't get to *finish that*—Miss Patty made him stop.

ISAAC. Stop talking, and let's go to the cave.

WILLA JO. We have to stay here.

LIZ. Oh… Okay. *(Brief pause. Trying again.)* How long is your visit? I hope it's all summer. I have to stay nearby so I can help Mama and there's no other kids except the ones I'm related to. I'm the oldest of five, and one on the way.

WILLA JO. I'm the oldest of two.

LIZ. Any on the way?

(LITTLE SISTER turns to WILLA JO.)

WILLA JO. …No. None on the way.

ISAAC *(to LITTLE SISTER)*. Can I see your picture?

WILLA JO. She— She doesn't want you to.

(PATTY comes to the door.)

PATTY. Well. What have we here?

LIZ. Hi, Miss Patty. We were just introducing ourselves.

ISAAC. Can we come inside?

PATTY. Won't your mother worry if you go into a stranger's house?

ISAAC. You're not a stranger— You're our across-the-street neighbor.

PATTY. I think your mother might worry. Come on, girls. Time for dinner.

WILLA JO. We just ate—.

PATTY. Your Uncle Hob didn't eat. We have to go inside now.

LIZ *(realizing they are not wanted)* Come on, Isaac. Time to go home.

ISAAC. Why?

LIZ. 'Cause I say so… Come on, we'll go to the cave.

ISAAC. Yippee.

(LIZ and ISAAC exit. PATTY comes down the stoop.)

WILLA JO. How come you get to use the porch door and we don't?

PATTY. Because I can come *out* as long as I go back *in* through the garage. Were they here for handouts?

WILLA JO. They came to play.

PATTY. There's other children in town more suitable.

(LITTLE SISTER gestures toward the FINGERSES; she likes them.)

WILLA JO. But… *(tentatively)* I think they're suitable.

PATTY. It's not suitable when dozens of people live in one house.

WILLA JO. There's only fourteen.

(LITTLE SISTER gestures the number fourteen repeatedly.)

PATTY *(over)*. Fourteen people! They're going to turn the street into a junkyard. What's she doing?

WILLA JO. That's the number fourteen. This means ten, plus four fingers equals fourteen.

PATTY. …Go 'round to your uncle, Little Sister.

(LITTLE SISTER exits. PATTY attempts to be calm.)

PATTY. Now, if you encourage her to be silent, she'll never talk.

WILLA JO. I don't encourage her.

PATTY. When you go out of your way to understand her hand signals, you encourage her.

WILLA JO. I don't mean to encourage, but I can't leave her alone in her silence. She would get lonesome.

PATTY. Willa Jo. ...Do you know why she stopped talking? *(Brief pause.)* If you know you have to tell.

WILLA JO *(lying)*. She's just sad, that's all.

PATTY. I'm sad, too. We're all plenty sad. I think it's high time she started talking again.

WILLA JO. She can't.

PATTY. She's willful like your mother.

WILLA JO. Mom's not—

PATTY. Don't tell me about Noreen, I've known her a sight longer than you have. Have you tried to make her talk?

WILLA JO. I try every day.

PATTY. You should just pinch her.

WILLA JO. We're not allowed to pinch.

PATTY. Or hold her upside down.

WILLA JO. For how long?!

PATTY. Until she gives up. She's doing it to get attention.

WILLA JO. Quietness don't get attention. I don't even know when she stopped talking that's how much attention she didn't get. You and Uncle Hob were there— you didn't notice—

PATTY. Your uncle and I were very busy taking care of other things.

WILLA JO. Everybody was. Everybody was busy and she just got quiet. Not for attention. She's too sad to talk, and that's the truth. And I hope nobody holds her upside down.

PATTY. All right, Willa Jo, nobody's going to hold her upside down. I just want her to talk. It's so nervous-making when she don't talk.

WILLA JO. I want her to talk. Mom wants her to talk. She can't talk. When she can talk, she will.

PATTY *(brief pause)*. Well, hasn't this been a fine first day.

WILLA JO. I think it's been a hard first day.

PATTY. I was being sarcastic.

WILLA JO. We're not allowed to be sarcastic.

PATTY. Adults are allowed. Go on in. See to your sister.

(WILLA JO exits through garage. PATTY snaps her shorts in frustration. HOB opens the porch door.)

PATTY. Don't come out that door, Hob.

HOB. I'm not going to. Honey? You all right?

PATTY. Oh, Hob. They hate me. They just hate me.

SCENE 2

(The backyard the next morning. LITTLE SISTER is in the tree with her painting. WILLA JO enters from the garage.)

WILLA JO. Little Sister? Where are you? *(Sees her, whispers.)* What are you doing up there? You are going to get us in so much trouble... *(Rhetorical.)* What did Mom say— What was the last thing she said? Sitting in a tree isn't being a *good girl.* Sitting in a tree ain't gonna make Aunt Patty *proud.*

(LITTLE SISTER gestures for WILLA JO to join her.)

WILLA JO. I'm calling the fire department. Tell them my cat is stuck up a tree.

(LITTLE SISTER insists.)

WILLA JO. Oh, all right. *(She climbs up to the tree limb.)* Going to scratch my legs all to pieces in these stupid shorts.

(HOB enters from the garage.)

HOB. You two watching birds?

WILLA JO. Tweet tweet.

HOB. My mistake—you are birds.

WILLA JO. Wanna come up?

HOB. It'd kill your Aunt Patty. She's afraid of heights.

WILLA JO. She don't have to come.

HOB. She's afraid of heights for everybody else, too. She won't even let me go up a ladder anymore. She worries a frightful lot about the people she loves.

WILLA JO *(doubting)*. Mom always says that.

HOB. She just wants you girls to be safe. And to be happy... Come on, before she gets back from the store. Come on down. *(He helps WILLA JO down.)* You, too, miss.

(LITTLE SISTER doesn't come down.)

WILLA JO *(excusing her)*. It *is* nice up there. A nice view.

HOB. Come on, hand me your picture. You need two hands to climb down.

WILLA JO. She didn't use two hands climbing up.

HOB. Willa Jo, please.

WILLA JO. But probably she should use them coming down. *(To LITTLE SISTER.)* Give it to me. I'll give it back.

(LITTLE SISTER hands WILLA JO the picture, comes down with HOB's help. The sound of a car.)

HOB. Just in the nick of time. We won't tell your aunt about the two of you going up the tree because...we don't want her to expire from "half a heart attack." Okay?

WILLA JO *(picking up on the joke)*. Okay, Uncle Hob. I wouldn't want her to get "half a heart attack."

PATTY *(off)*. Help me with these bags, Hob.

HOB. What's for lunch?

PATTY *(entering with grocery bags)*. We're having a spontaneous party is what. I ran into the Wainwrights at the store.

HOB. Is this about that dang ladies' club of hers?

PATTY. Well, it won't hurt my chances if Lucy brings her daughter over for a visit.

HOB. Since when are the two of you on a first-name basis?

PATTY. Well, I was standing behind her at the counter and she came up forty-five cents short to pay her bill, so I said, oh don't return that can of beans, I'll get it, Mrs Wainwright. At which point we had a nice conversation about the girls. She is very anxious for Cynthia to meet them.

WILLA JO. Can the Fingerses come to the party?

PATTY. No Fingerses.

HOB. Patty— *(Big sigh.)* Never mind.

PATTY. Hob, you know those children aren't suitable—

HOB. I'm taking these in. *(He exits with the groceries to garage.)*

PATTY. Let me see, turn around. *(WILLA JO turns around.)* I guess these clothes will have to do.

WILLA JO. What do you mean? These are the clothes you bought us—

PATTY. Willa Jo, please don't sass—

WILLA JO. I'm not—

PATTY. And make sure your sister stays clean. I'm going to put out some cookies. Hob—

(PATTY exits through garage. LITTLE SISTER heads toward the tree.)

WILLA JO. No! Come on over here. We'll just stay nice and quiet. And clean.

(The girls stand for a second. Then LITTLE SISTER starts to rearrange the yard gnomes into conversational groups.)

WILLA JO. What...? Oh, gee... Okay... Let me help so you don't get dirty. *(She helps.)* Aunt Patty is not going to approve.

(LITTLE SISTER gestures for WILLA JO to talk for a gnome.)

WILLA JO. Talk for him yourself.

(LITTLE SISTER turns away.)

WILLA JO. I just…I just don't know what these particular type of yard people say… Okay. *(She talks in gnome voices.)* "So. What do you think about our owners?" "I like them a sight more than the people at the yard-fairy factory." "And I surely love their visiting nieces!"

(LITTLE SISTER hugs a gnome.)

WILLA JO. Can I put them back before we get into trouble?

LUCY *(off)*. Come on, darling, they're 'round the back.

WILLA JO. Too late. Here comes the company. Behave, okay?

(LUCY and CYNTHIA enter.)

LUCY. Hello, there.

WILLA JO. Hi. I'll go get Aunt Patty.

LUCY. No need, dear. This is Cynthia. Cynthia, these are Miss Patty's nieces, Willa Jo and Jo Ann.

WILLA JO. We call her Little Sister.

LUCY. Isn't that sweet. Helloooo, Patty.

(LUCY heads for the porch door.)

WILLA JO. Oh no, you can't.

LUCY. What, dear?

WILLA JO. You mustn't. You really mustn't.

PATTY *(enters with cookies)*. Hello, Lucy. Hello, Cynthia, dear.

WILLA JO. She was going to come in the door.

PATTY. Well, of course Mrs. Wainwright is going to come in the door. Whatever are you thinking of, Willa Jo?

WILLA JO. But, you—

PATTY. The rules for the children don't apply to the adults. Here, you go, girls. Two cookies each. *(To LUCY.)* I don't want them to overeat sugar, Lucy. You know how riled they get when they eat too many sweets. What—? What have you done with my garden gnomes? Oh, never mind. Be careful with things that aren't yours, girls. Be careful you don't break them. Come on inside, Lucy. I've got some cake for us.

LUCY. That'll be lovely.

PATTY. You girls, play nice. Mind your manners.

(The ladies go inside through the porch door. After a brief pause, CYNTHIA takes all the cookies from the plate.)

WILLA JO. What—?

CYNTHIA. I really like this kind of cookie.

WILLA JO. Two, we each get two.

CYNTHIA. Two is not enough for me.

WILLA JO. We're supposed to share.

CYNTHIA. Yes, but I'm the guest, and it's your responsibility to make sure I have a good time. I won't have a good enough time unless I eat six cookies.

WILLA JO. But that doesn't leave any for us.

CYNTHIA. But you live here, and here is where the rest of the cookies are, and we don't get cookies anymore at my house. It's good manners to let me have them all.

(LITTLE SISTER crosses to CYNTHIA.)

CYNTHIA. What is she doing? Tell your sister she can't have a cookie.

(LITTLE SISTER gestures her sign for "half.")

WILLA JO. Can she have half a cookie?

CYNTHIA. That would be unsanitary. I have already touched them all.

WILLA JO. Never mind. She doesn't want a cookie. You don't want a cookie, Little Sister.

(LITTLE SISTER looks closely at a cookie.)

CYNTHIA. What is she looking at?

WILLA JO. …She's looking at your dress is all.

CYNTHIA. It looks to me like she's looking at a cookie.

WILLA JO. Well, she's not. *(Making this up.)* We never saw a dress like that up close. It looks like a dress from a storybook. It is fascinating to her.

CYNTHIA. Old-fashioned is in style now. This is very in style.

WILLA JO. Oh, it's really pretty.

CYNTHIA. Yes, and it's in style.

WILLA JO. Kind of fancy for the summer.

CYNTHIA. A lady is always prepared to delight the viewer no matter what the cost to her comfort. I'm going to sit over here to prevent my appearance from getting harmed.

(CYNTHIA flounces over to a gnome and sits on it. LITTLE SISTER flounces along next to her.)

CYNTHIA. Tell her to get away from me.

WILLA JO. You can tell her.

CYNTHIA *(whisper)*. I don't know how to speak to her.

WILLA JO. You speak to her like you speak to anybody else.

CYNTHIA *(whisper)*. Isn't she deaf?

WILLA JO. She isn't deaf. She isn't anything at all. Just tell her.

CYNTHIA *(too loudly)*. Go stand over there.

(LITTLE SISTER bends over as if she were a gnome whose back was aching from the weight of CYNTHIA WAINWRIGHT.)

CYNTHIA. What is she doing? Is she making fun of me? What are you smiling about?

WILLA JO *(scuffling)*. She's not making fun—it's a…private family joke is what.

CYNTHIA. You are supposed to tell private family jokes to the family *in private*. Don't you people know anything at all?

WILLA JO. We know plenty.

CYNTHIA. You know nothing. You are two know-nothings.

(Brief insulted pause, then LITTLE SISTER gestures for WILLA JO to talk for the gnome. WILLA JO's reluctance to insult CYNTHIA is gone.)

WILLA JO. "Oh my back is so sore. What's on my back? Somebody musta put some thousand-pound something on my back."

CYNTHIA. Stop it. Stop talking like that.

WILLA JO. "Oh I wish they would take it off me before I get squashed to death from the weight of it."

CYNTHIA. I am not a thousand pounds. It is bad manners to talk about somebody else's weight, but you don't know that because you know nothing. You are trash. You get to live here out of the good graces of your aunt. Otherwise you would go to an orphanage.

WILLA JO. Don't say that.

CYNTHIA. Your aunt had to buy you new clothes because your old ones are rags.

WILLA JO. Our old ones are fine.

CYNTHIA. I shouldn't have expected anything better. People like you don't have manners to mind.

WILLA JO. You're the one took all the cookies—

CYNTHIA. And if you had manners you would have given them to me without a second thought. Your aunt will be the *laughingstock* of the county once we tell everybody about you. She won't be able to hold up her head.

(WILLA JO is struck by this possibility. LITTLE SISTER starts her gnome backache walk again.)

WILLA JO. Stop it, Little Sister. Really. Stop it, now. *(To CYNTHIA.)* She's sorry. And I'm sorry, too. We forgot our manners for a minute because…because we just got here and forgot them. But now we remember them, we won't forget them again. Okay? So there's no cause for you to make my aunt a laughingstock.

CYNTHIA. I want more cookies.

WILLA JO. I don't know if Aunt Patty will give us more.

(PATTY and LUCY come to the door.)

PATTY. Girls, Miss Lucy has offered to give you a charm school lesson. Isn't that wonderful?

WILLA JO. What's charm school?

LUCY. Where we teach you how to act like little ladies.

CYNTHIA. I don't know, Mommy, you need to know *manners* before you learn *charm*. As a matter of fact—

WILLA JO. Aunt Patty…Cynthia didn't get her fair share of the cookies.

PATTY. How did that happen?

WILLA JO. Because…I ate too many.

PATTY. Willa Jo— How many cookies did you eat?

WILLA JO. I ate them all. Every single one of them.

PATTY. Oh my, oh my word. I'll get you a whole new plate, Cynthia. Lucy, you see how badly these girls need charm school?

SCENE 3

(A few hours later. The cave. An underground room reinforced with boards. Clip-on lights; an extension cord

snakes through the entrance. LIZ reads in an old chair. ISAAC digs and sings in the fashion of Hank Williams.)

ISAAC *(sings a mining song.)* "I got the coal miner blu ooo ooo ooo ooo ooo ooo ooo ooos."

(Enter WILLA JO then LITTLE SISTER with her rolled-up picture. LITTLE SISTER hesitates.)

LIZ. Hey, hi!

ISAAC. Hi! This is the cave; it's a mine; I'm a miner. *(Sings.)* "Ooo ooo ooo ooo ooo ooo ooo ooo ooo ooo oooos."

LIZ. I didn't think you'd come.

ISAAC. The cave is irresistible.

WILLA JO. Come on in, Little Sister.

ISAAC. Everybody loves a cave.

(LITTLE SISTER exits.)

WILLA JO. What—? Oh, man. I gotta go. Listen, I'm sorry about my—I'm sorry about everything. Bye.

(WILLA JO follows LITTLE SISTER.)

LIZ. Can't you stay— Bye… Well. That's the shortest cave visit on record.

ISAAC. I never heard of anybody not liking a cave.

LIZ. You've heard of it now.

(WILLA JO and LITTLE SISTER, without her painting, reenter.)

WILLA JO. Hi, again.

ISAAC *(to LIZ)*. See?

LIZ. Hope you can stay longer this time.

ISAAC. I'm digging and digging. I'm a miner. If you want to stay you have to dig.

LIZ. No, they don't.

(LITTLE SISTER starts to help him.)

ISAAC. Here. We do it a spoonful at a time because we don't want the walls to cave in on us. *(Realizes.)* That's why they call it a cave because the walls *cave in on you*. Dig there and put the dirt in this bucket.

WILLA JO. It's not really going to cave in, is it?

LIZ. Don't worry. Uncle Larry knows what he's doing. He built caves like this in Vietnam, so they'd have safe headquarters for the officers.

WILLA JO. Your uncle fought in the war?

LIZ. Uncle Larry was a soldier, but now he's too shell-shocked. The walls are shored up real good. *(Whisper.)* How did you talk her into coming back?

WILLA JO. I didn't. She didn't want to bring her picture down is all.

LIZ. Can we see it?

WILLA JO. She won't even show it to me.

LIZ. How was your visit with Cynthia Wainwright?

WILLA JO. You saw her?

ISAAC. Nobody plays with Cynthia Wainwright.

LIZ. Isaac, be nice.

ISAAC. *She's* not nice.

WILLA JO. She called us names. She said my aunt wouldn't be able to hold up her head on account of us.

LIZ. Don't worry about what Cynthia Wainwright says.

WILLA JO. I don't want to cause my aunt shame.

LIZ. Really, nobody listens to her. She's a stuck-up nothing.

WILLA JO. We have to get a charm lesson from her mom.

LIZ. Could I get it, too?

WILLA JO. Why would you want to?

LIZ. I need to be a model. Like these ones. *(Shows magazine.)*

WILLA JO. How come?

LIZ. They're tall. I'm gonna be tall like my daddy. I need to be around other tall ladies so I feel more normal.

WILLA JO. They're sure tall.

LIZ. Yes. And models need to know charm. And how to walk in high heels.

WILLA JO. You wouldn't think they need high heels.

LIZ. I know—it must be some rule. I don't like Mrs. Wainwright, but she knows all the charm rules.

ISAAC. It says "for rent."

LIZ. What says "for rent"?

ISAAC. The charm school. It has a sign out front. I saw it when me and Mama went to the Laundromat.

WILLA JO. I wonder where we're gonna meet?

ISAAC. Can meet here. We can all get charmed. *(He walks like a model.)* Pretty good, huh?

LIZ. You're a miner, not a model.

ISAAC. *Lots* of miners work two jobs. *(He goes back to digging.)*

LIZ. You want to sit down?

WILLA JO. No thanks. Kind of creepy down here.

LIZ. Yeah! Mama won't let the little ones come down, so I usually get it to myself. I read my magazine while Uncle Larry makes improvements. He used to work in the mines.

WILLA JO. My dad was a miner. In the coalfields until they closed down.

LIZ. What's he do now?

WILLA JO. Well…I don't know exactly. But it's really a very good job. The one he has now. It's very important.

LIZ. He's lucky he found a job. A lot of miners are still out of work.

(Unseen, LITTLE SISTER listens to WILLA JO spin her lie.)

WILLA JO. Yeah. But my daddy, he's real smart, so he got a new job right off. In another town.

LIZ. Are y'all gonna move there?

WILLA JO. We are…eventually we are. But right now he's got to get everything settled. Before he uproots us. He don't want to uproot us prematurely.

(WILLA JO sees LITTLE SISTER who has crept nearby.)

WILLA JO. What are you doing here? Go be a miner.

ISAAC. We are moles now. We are digging our mole tunnel. *(He squeaks and digs.)*

WILLA JO. Go on. Go be a mole. Don't be standing around looking at me like that.

(LITTLE SISTER joins ISAAC. She does not squeak.)

ISAAC. We must find food for our baby moles.

LIZ. There's cookies left in the bag, Mr. Mole.

ISAAC. My powerful mole nose smells mole food in this bag, Mrs. Mole. We will take it back to our tunnel.

LIZ. Leave some for us.

(ISAAC and LITTLE SISTER take cookies and return to digging.)

LIZ. Here.

WILLA JO. Thanks. Cynthia Wainwright ate all our cookies.

LIZ. Take as many as you want.

WILLA JO. Your mom give you the whole bag?

LIZ. She knows we won't eat them all.

WILLA JO. That's what my mom would say.

LIZ. Is she coming for a visit, too?

WILLA JO. She stayed back at home…because…because she has to keep working…on next year's Mother's Day.

LIZ. What's she do for Mother's Day?

WILLA JO. She makes greeting cards. She paints pictures and then the company turns them into cards. That's what Little Sister's carrying around, one of them greeting-card paintings… She really loves her work.

LIZ. Maybe she can keep her job when y'all move.

WILLA JO. When we move where?

LIZ. When you move to be with your dad.

WILLA JO. Oh!… I don't know.

LIZ *(looking around)*. Sure. She can do the paintings and mail them to the greeting card company. Do you guys get to stay all summer?

WILLA JO. We'll have to see. When our dad sends for us.

LIZ *(picks up a soda bottle)*. Isaac, what did you do with the pop?
ISAAC. I didn't bring any.
LIZ. Here. Have a swig to wash down the cookie.
WILLA JO. …What is it?
LIZ. It's just water, even though it's in a pop bottle.

(LIZ extends the bottle toward WILLA JO. LITTLE SISTER grabs it and pours it out.)

LIZ. Hey—
WILLA JO. Little Sister—
LIZ. Give it to me—
WILLA JO. Leave her. Leave her alone.

(LITTLE SISTER starts to shake. WILLA JO comforts her.)

WILLA JO. It's okay. I didn't drink any. It's okay.

(LITTLE SISTER buries herself into WILLA JO; sobs.)

WILLA JO. I'm fine, Little Sister. Shhhhh.
ISAAC. I didn't do it. It isn't my fault.
LIZ. I know. Hush, now.
WILLA JO. We have to go. I'm sorry about the water.

(WILLA JO and LITTLE SISTER exit.)

ISAAC. What's wrong with them?
LIZ. Something powerful bad.

SCENE 4

(The backyard. The next day. CYNTHIA, WILLA JO and LITTLE SISTER are balancing books on their heads.)

CYNTHIA. You look like a zombie from a movie, Willa Jo. You have to stand up straight but relax at the same time.

(LITTLE SISTER's book falls.)

CYNTHIA. You turned too fast. Part of being a lady is never being startled. A lady always remains calm.

WILLA JO. Come here by me, Little Sister.

CYNTHIA. No, she has to balance it herself.

WILLA JO. Who makes up these rules?

CYNTHIA. They're common knowledge. Your shoes are making you unbalanced. It isn't possible to walk like a lady in sandals.

WILLA JO *(insulted)*. Class is over.

CYNTHIA. People like you always give up when it gets hard.

WILLA JO. I don't care what you say about us. Nobody listens to you.

(LITTLE SISTER sniffs and holds her nose.)

WILLA JO. Your dress needs washing.

CYNTHIA. It so happens you can't wash a dress like this. You have to take it to the dry cleaners, and that costs money.

WILLA JO. Well, better take up a collection because your dress is overdue.

CYNTHIA. That remark…is without charm.

WILLA JO. Maybe we'll learn remarks with charm in lesson two.

CYNTHIA. My mommy will never teach you lesson two because you can't pass lesson one.

WILLA JO. Maybe your mommy isn't going to teach anybody anything anymore.

CYNTHIA. What is that supposed to mean?

WILLA JO. It means where's the school? We're in a backyard.

CYNTHIA. The landlord is…painting the charm school… So we can't use it now. Besides, charm is for everywhere.

WILLA JO. You sure you just didn't forget to pay the rent?

CYNTHIA. Why do you say that?

WILLA JO. I don't see any other paying customers. Just me and Little Sister. Maybe the charm school is *for rent*. Landlord looking for new tenants.

CYNTHIA. You're not paying customers. My mommy is giving you this lesson out of the goodness of her heart so your aunt doesn't have to suffer the humiliation of having charmless nieces.

WILLA JO. Stop calling us names—

CYNTHIA. My mommy is trying…is trying above all else… *(new tactic)* …to give your aunt every opportunity to get into the Ladies' Social League.

WILLA JO. What's that?

CYNTHIA. It's an exclusive ladies' club and your aunt is dying to get into it. But she will never get in if her nieces don't have charm. *(Brief pause.)* Your aunt wants to be in this club more than anything.

WILLA JO. ...Put the book on your head, Little Sister.

(LITTLE SISTER can't believe it.)

WILLA JO. Come on, do it.

CYNTHIA. Yes, do it. If you do everything I say, your aunt might be allowed into the club.

(PATTY and LUCY come out the porch door.)

LUCY. Why aren't you girls walking? Come here, Jo Ann. I'll put that back on your head for you.

WILLA JO. Don't just stand there. Do what Miss Lucy says. Go on. She's going to help you get it right.

(LITTLE SISTER doesn't move.)

PATTY. You'd have more luck balancing the book if you put down that picture, Little—Jo Ann.

WILLA JO. Give it to me. Little Sister, give me the picture, right now. *(WILLA JO takes the picture and puts it on the ground.)* Now, we're going to show Aunt Patty how much improved our posture is. Okay? Okay!?

(LITTLE SISTER nods.)

WILLA JO. We're going to make Aunt Patty proud of us. Because that's what Mom wants us to do. Understand? Now walk.

(WILLA JO and LITTLE SISTER walk with the books on their heads.)

LUCY. Why, look how straight and tall. Willa Jo looks three inches taller just because she's standing up straight. Don't stand on your tiptoes, Jo Ann. That's not the way to look taller. *(She demonstrates.)* Stand tall, relax the shoulders, come on, Cynthia, you too, swing the arms, do not swing the fanny, we are all lovely ladies walking down the boulevard. Come to a halt ever so slowly, never surprise yourself, you could topple right over. "Hello, Mr. Smith." Repeat after me, "Hello, Mr. Smith."

CYNTHIA/WILLA JO. "Hello, Mr. Smith."

LUCY. "Why, I'd be delighted to dance this dance with you."

CYNTHIA/WILLA JO. "Why, I'd be delighted to dance this dance with you."

LUCY. "Let me check my dance card."

CYNTHIA/WILLA JO. "Let me check my dance card."

(LUCY picks up the painting to move it out of the way. LITTLE SISTER snatches it away from her.)

PATTY. Little Sister! You almost knocked down Miss Lucy. Now apologize.

LUCY. Never mind, Patty. It's all right, dear.

PATTY. Go on inside. Tell Uncle Hob to get you some milk.

WILLA JO. I'll tell him—

PATTY. You stay right there. Little Sister, go on in. Go on.

(LITTLE SISTER goes inside with her painting.)

LUCY. Don't give it another thought, Patty. Willa Jo, you're doing fine. Isn't she doing fine, Cynthia?

CYNTHIA. Yes, Mommy. She's a natural.

LUCY. You must sign her up for the full series of lessons, Patty. It would do her a world of good.

PATTY. You'd take her on?

LUCY. *Your* niece? Of course, I will. The entire course is only thirty dollars. If you like, I'll take Jo Ann, too.

CYNTHIA. But she has special problems, Mommy.

LUCY. Yes, I know, dear. I'd have to charge you more for Jo Ann. It's only fair.

PATTY. I don't know—

LUCY *(quickly)*. I'd take them both for seventy dollars.

CYNTHIA. And the kit, Mommy.

LUCY. Oh, I almost forgot. Each girl must purchase her own toiletry kit. Oh! I believe I have one with me. *(Gets it from her purse.)* The girl gets schooled in the use of each of the implements: nail file, emery board, cuticle stick, complexion brush. They're only five dollars. And the carrying case is so handy.

WILLA JO. Why would I want to be carrying around that stuff?

CYNTHIA. They are the implements a lady needs to stay prissy.

LUCY. To stay *pristine*, dear.

PATTY. All right, Lucy. Take 'em on. Take them both on.

ISAAC *(from off)*. Hi, we're coming to your yard.

PATTY. Oh, what now? Willa Jo, did you invite them?

WILLA JO. I don't know, I might have— Yes, I think I did.

(Enter LIZ and ISAAC. He has flowers.)

WILLA JO. Hi, Liz, Hey, Isaac.

LIZ. Howdy, Willa Jo. Cynthia. Hi, Miss Lucy, Miss Patty. Y'all practice the walk yet?

CYNTHIA. Mommy showed it already.

ISAAC *(hands PATTY flowers)*. These are for you.

PATTY. Well…goodness.

ISAAC. I picked them in my yard.

WILLA JO. They're really nice, Isaac.

ISAAC. They're called dandelions.

PATTY. Yes, I know that.

ISAAC. They're a very famous flower. Named after a lion. You know what else? You can eat the leaves. But you don't have to, you can just put them in water.

(HOB and LITTLE SISTER, without painting, enter from garage.)

HOB. Did we hear somebody talking about a dance card?

LIZ. Hi, Mr. Hob.

ISAAC. Hi, Mr. Hob.

HOB. Isaac, Lizzy.

PATTY. Hob, you're not interested in charm school.

HOB. I am if there's dancing.

PATTY. You don't like to dance.

HOB. I do like to dance. It's you doesn't like it. Come on Little Sister, let's try a waltz.

(LITTLE SISTER and HOB waltz. He hums a waltz count.)

ISAAC. I'm not dancing in front of people.
LIZ. Yes you are. Come on.

(LIZ and ISAAC waltz and hum.)

HOB. Thank you so much, Miss Little Sister, for saving a place on your card for me.
PATTY. How'd you get her picture away from her?
HOB. Patty— It's fine. Okay?!
PATTY. Well...*we* couldn't get it away from her is all I'm saying.
CYNTHIA *(to LIZ)*. How come you know how to waltz?
LIZ. We have music every Friday. Mama plays the piano and the rest of us dance and sing.
PATTY. We've certainly heard it.
HOB *(quickly, to cover)*. And we enjoy it! And we're so sorry when you stop at nine o'clock.
ISAAC. Mama won't play past nine for fear of disturbing people.
CYNTHIA. We have fussy neighbors, too. Always telling Mommy and Daddy to stop yelling.
LUCY. Cynthia, enough. What she means is...

(ISAAC steps on LIZ's foot.)

LIZ. Ouch.
ISAAC. I said I didn't want to.

(HOB brings the waltz to an elegant end.)

HOB. Thank you, Miss Little Sister, for saving a place on your dance card for me.

ISAAC. Hey, Little Sister. You want to go over to the cave while the big kids do dancing?

(LITTLE SISTER nods.)

PATTY. She's not going to any cave.
WILLA JO. It's really safe, Aunt Patty.
PATTY. What do you mean, it's really safe?
LUCY. I've heard about Larry Fingers' cave.
PATTY. Larry Fingers? Oh, my goodness.
LIZ. It's a great cave. Uncle Larry wouldn't put us in harm's way.
CYNTHIA. Can I go see it, Mommy?
ISAAC. You're not invited.
LIZ. Isaac! You can come any time you like, Cynthia.
LUCY. No, she may not. You may not go in a cave.
PATTY. And you two may not go in a cave.
HOB. You can play right here in our yard.
ISAAC. Yippee! *(He talks to the yard gnomes.)* Hello, Mr. Yard Fairy. How are you and your friends? *(Counts them.)* One two three four five six seven. How are the seven yard fairies?

(LITTLE SISTER joins him.)

ISAAC *(talks for the gnomes)*. "Do you hate to dance?" "I hate to dance." "I like to dig in the mine."
PATTY. Careful, please be careful. They're not toys.
ISAAC. If they're not toys, what are they?
HOB *(brief pause)*. Patty? Answer the lad.

PATTY. They are yard decorations. So people know our house. I can say, the house with "the gnomes in the yard."

ISAAC. Then how come they're in the backyard and not the front yard?

HOB. Patty?

PATTY. ...Lucy, let's take a look at that kit for the girls. The toiletry kit.

ISAAC. A toilet kit? It's a toilet kit? With tiny toilet paper and a tiny toilet?

CYNTHIA. Not toilet—

LUCY. Isn't that cute? *Toiletry* is how a lady refers to the items she uses to keep herself tidy. I provide these kits for my students for a nominal fee.

LIZ. I have that kit! I sent away for it. A dollar-fifty plus postage.

LUCY. Well, I'm sure they're not the same. These are quality items in this kit.

HOB. Thirty-five cents tops. You got over-charged, Lizzy.

PATTY. Well...the case must cost something, Hob.

LUCY. Come on, Cynthia. I think this lesson is over.

PATTY. It's not over, Lucy. Liz and Isaac are just going home.

ISAAC. We are?

LIZ. I'm sorry, Miss Patty. We'll go. I just wanted to see the charm school lesson.

HOB *(quickly)*. What's your interest in charm, Lizzy?

WILLA JO. She's going to be a model.

CYNTHIA. She can't be a model. Mommy, how can she be a model?

HOB. She'll be a lovely model. Show us some modeling, Lizzie.

ISAAC. She knows the walk.

HOB. Well, show us all the walk.

(LIZ demonstrates a model walk.)

LUCY. I must say. That's very interesting, Liz. But perhaps it is just a little too vulgar for a lady.

WILLA JO. It's just how *you* did it.

LUCY. I did not swing my hips in that suggestive fashion.

WILLA JO. It's like she learned it right from your charm school.

PATTY. Willa Jo—

LUCY. I teach my students how to be young ladies. I protect them from their more vulgar tendencies.

HOB. Miss Lucy—! Patty…the girls have had enough charm for one day.

PATTY. Yes, Hob, I think you're right.

HOB. Let's let the children play, and we'll go back inside and have some more of that cream cake, which was quite charming itself.

PATTY. Come on, Lucy, let's go inside.

HOB. We using the porch door again?

PATTY. Hob… Of course we're using the porch door. What possible other door would we be using?

(The ladies go inside.)

HOB *(conspiratorially)*. I get to use the porch door, Little Sister. Y'all go ahead now, play with those yard gnomes all you want. *(He goes inside.)*

ISAAC. Yippee.

(ISAAC and LITTLE SISTER play with the gnomes.)

CYNTHIA. You'll probably break them.

ISAAC. "For rent, for rent."

LIZ. Isaac, please…What all you doing for the summer, Cynthia?

CYNTHIA. We're very busy. *(Pointedly.)* My mommy has meetings every day at her club. About who can get in. And who *can't*.

WILLA JO. I hope she'll let my Aunt Patty get in.

CYNTHIA. Until a few days ago, your aunt had a very good chance of getting into the club.

WILLA JO. I hope she still has a good chance.

CYNTHIA. Her chances have gotten a lot worse. As a matter of fact, your aunt will never get in as long as you're visiting her.

LIZ. It's impossible to be nice to you, Cynthia.

CYNTHIA. Their aunt rescued them from the gutter. They are guttersnipes.

LIZ *(to WILLA JO)*. Don't take this from her.

WILLA JO. Never mind, Liz—

LIZ. Call your daddy.

WILLA JO *(shocked)*. What? Why?

LIZ *(over)*. Tell him you need a rescue from the Wainwrights.

(LITTLE SISTER joins WILLA JO.)

CYNTHIA. She can't call her daddy.

LIZ. Pick you up, get you out of here.

CYNTHIA. She can't call her daddy because nobody knows where he is.

ISAAC. Willa Jo knows exactly where he is.

CYNTHIA. Nobody knows where he is. They haven't heard from him in a year. He left them high and dry.

(Brief pause. LIZ looks at WILLA JO.)

ISAAC. You're lying—

LIZ. We gotta go, Isaac. We gotta go home and help Mama.

ISAAC. Goodbye, Willa Jo. I'm sorry she said those mean things about your daddy.

LIZ. I said let's go, now come on.

(ISAAC and LIZ exit.)

CYNTHIA. I'm gonna get me some cake. *(She goes inside.)*

(LITTLE SISTER points toward the Fingerses.)

WILLA JO. I know. I'll go talk to her, but I don't know what I'm gonna say.

(PATTY comes out the porch door. In a whisper.)

PATTY. What did you do? Cynthia says you were mean to her.

WILLA JO. She told Liz and Isaac that our daddy run off and left us high and dry.

PATTY *(defensive)*. What are you talking about?

WILLA JO. Did you tell them about Daddy? 'Cause I sure didn't tell anybody and Little Sister ain't talking.

PATTY. I didn't say anything more than what was true.
WILLA JO. They don't need to know about us—
PATTY. Are you talking back to me?
WILLA JO. No, I'm talking *front* to you.
PATTY *(gasps)*. You… If I didn't have company—
WILLA JO. Yeah, you don't want to be rude to the Wainwrights. You better get in there and serve them up some more cake.

(PATTY is speechless. She huffs and puffs, then snaps her shorts.)

PATTY. I will talk to you after the company has gone home. You stay right here. You do not leave this yard for any reason.

(PATTY exits. WILLA JO snaps her shorts in PATTY's direction.)

WILLA JO *(to LITTLE SISTER)*. Go get some cake.

(LITTLE SISTER shakes her head.)

WILLA JO. Then don't, I don't care.

(WILLA JO exits, leaving LITTLE SISTER astonished.)

SCENE 5

(A few minutes later. The cave. LIZ is alone. She looks at her magazine. WILLA JO enters.)

WILLA JO. Hi.

LIZ. Your aunt's gonna be fit to be tied.

WILLA JO. I'm not staying long.

LIZ. Yeah? You need to rush back to the Wainwrights?

WILLA JO. Are you being sarcastic?

LIZ. I am.

WILLA JO. I'm not allowed to be.

LIZ. Me neither, except in the cave.

WILLA JO. ...You know, you did the walk *exactly* like Mrs. Wainwright. Except yours was better. *(Brief pause.)* What Cynthia said was true. About my dad.

LIZ. I thought we were friends.

WILLA JO. I'm sorry. I should have trusted you.

LIZ. I guess you had your reasons. *(Brief pause.)* Maybe you better go home before you rile up your aunt.

WILLA JO. Dad left us to find work. At first he called every Saturday. Then one Saturday he didn't. Then he never did again... Then our baby sister died.

LIZ. Oh, Willa—

WILLA JO. It wasn't anybody's fault. We were all missing Dad so much, Mom decided we needed a diversion. We drove out to the carnival was laid out in an old soybean field. There were rides and games but there wasn't any faucet water on account of it was in a field. Me and Little Sister and Mom drank pop, but babies can't drink pop, they need water and juice and milk and refrigerators— *(She is breaking down.)* We were going to have to leave—we were going to have to leave and go to town for Baby to get a drink—

LIZ. Willa Jo, it's okay, you don't have to tell me—

WILLA JO *(over)*. We so didn't want to leave. Little Sister said, "Oh please, Mom, please don't make us leave, I'm having just the best time." We asked one of the workers, and he had water in a bottle, a bottle like the one over there. Mom filled up Baby's bottle with the water and Baby drank it all up. Baby died that night. She died from the bad water from the bottle. I think that's why Little Sister won't talk. She's afraid to say one more thing.

LIZ. I'm sorry, Willa Jo, I'm so sorry. You don't have to apologize to me for anything.

PATTY *(off)*. Willa Jo? Willa Jo, are you in that cave? *(The girls are silent. To herself.)* I swear—Hob? Hob… *(Her voice fades off.)*

WILLA JO. I gotta go.

LIZ. I'm not mad at you in the slightest. I swear I'm not.

WILLA JO. Thanks.

SCENE 6

(The backyard, immediately following. PATTY enters. LITTLE SISTER is up the tree with her painting.)

PATTY. Willa Jo, you inside there? *(Turns and sees LITTLE SISTER.)* What—oh, goodness, don't—don't move a muscle. What are you doing? I turn my back on you for one second— Do you want me to have half a heart attack right here and now?

(LITTLE SISTER gestures a query involving her gesture for "half.")

PATTY. What? What does that mean? I swear if you don't come down… One, two… Little Sister, when your uncle gets back, he's going to whale the tar out of you. *(To herself.)* What am I saying?… Little Sister, don't you see how upset I am? Don't you see how much I need you to get out of that tree? Bad enough I can't find your sister. Do you want me to have to call your mother?

(LITTLE SISTER nods.)

PATTY. No, you don't. I'm calling the fire department, that's who I'm calling.

(Enter WILLA JO.)

WILLA JO. I'll get her down.

PATTY. Young lady, where have you been? Did I not tell you, did I not say you were forbidden to leave this yard? Do you know where your uncle is? He's combing the streets in our car shouting your name like you're some lost dog. What do you think people are going to think of me I can't keep track of my niece?

WILLA JO. They won't think nothing of you. They'll just think you have a trashy niece.

PATTY. And you don't think that reflects on me—? Wait a minute. Are you being sarcastic, young lady?

WILLA JO *(brief pause, then lies)*. No.

PATTY. What am I supposed to do with you? Lucy Wainwright brings her daughter over to meet you and you *shun* her. You send her inside to be with the grownups.

WILLA JO. She's a snake—

PATTY. She is a lovely, mindful little girl.

WILLA JO. She's a cookie thief and she don't wash. The only reason I don't sock her into tomorrow is `cause of that stupid club.

PATTY. You will never sock anybody into tomorrow or any other day. You hear me?

WILLA JO. If you don't get in the club, it won't be on account of me.

PATTY. Why…I'll have you know I invited the Wainwrights for *your* benefit. You and your sister.

WILLA JO. Well it don't benefit us!

PATTY. I—I—

(PATTY snaps her shorts. WILLA JO snaps her shorts back at her.)

WILLA JO. There. Whatever that means.

PATTY. Oh, that's it. That is just the last of it, Miss Willa Jo Dean. I am going to set down some rules, and you are going to follow each and every one of them. Is that clear?

WILLA JO. I've been trying to follow your rules since we got here.

PATTY. Don't talk back. I'm going to make some telephone calls and see if I can locate your Uncle Hob. See you get her out of the tree. And get that picture away from her. I'm sick of seeing it in her hand. Then go to bed, just go to bed. *(PATTY exits to garage.)*

WILLA JO. Come down now! Give me that—

(LITTLE SISTER hands her the picture and climbs down.)

WILLA JO. What were you doing up there? Tell me. Why were you in the tree making everything worse?… Fine. I guess it's high time I see what all the fuss is about.

(LITTLE SISTER tries to get it back.)

WILLA JO. What? I should just give this back? So you can make Aunt Patty mad and get me in worse trouble? *(WILLA JO opens the picture. Her anger fades away.)* Well. Will you look at that. Looks just like her.

(LITTLE SISTER holds it so WILLA JO can see it properly. It is a painting of Baby, Smiling Baby with wings, Baby in the clouds.)

WILLA JO. Oh yeah. It looks better from faraway. Just like Mom says. Is that why you went in the tree? Get Baby closer to the sky?

(LITTLE SISTER nods.)

WILLA JO. And you didn't want her in the cave because it was the wrong direction!

(LITTLE SISTER nods.)

WILLA JO. Well, I think getting closer to the sky is a fine idea. I know where there's a whole lot of sky we can get right close to. Tonight we're gonna find us some sky.

END OF ACT ONE

ACT TWO

(The next morning. The roof. LITTLE SISTER sleeps, hugging her painting. WILLA JO is standing and smiling at the sky. She sits next to LITTLE SISTER to wake her up.)

WILLA JO. Hey. Hey, sleepyhead. You already missed the sunrise. But you mustn't miss this perfect perfect cloud.

(LITTLE SISTER sits up.)

WILLA JO. Careful… Remember watching the sunrise with Mom?

(LITTLE SISTER nods.)

WILLA JO. I thought she lost her whole mind staying up 'til dawn. Then I figured it out. Baby died at sunrise. Mom stayed up to say goodbye… You hungry?

(LITTLE SISTER nods.)

WILLA JO. You want to go inside now?

(LITTLE SISTER shakes her head.)

WILLA JO. Okay, but we can't stay up here forever.

(LITTLE SISTER gestures; she wants to stay forever.)

WILLA JO. We can't. There's no refrigerator, for one thing. No bathroom, for another. I personally would like to go in and pee.

(LITTLE SISTER shakes her head.)

WILLA JO. Okay.

(Brief pause. The girls watch the cloud pass over the sun as the FINGERSES sneak into the yard.)

LIZ *(to ISAAC)*. You be quiet, now.

ISAAC *(seeing WILLA JO and LITTLE SISTER)*. Mama was right.

LIZ *(whispers)*. Willa Jo, what are you doing up there?

WILLA JO. Watching the sun come up.

LIZ. Your aunt know you're up there?

WILLA JO. Yep. She thought the air would do us good.

LIZ. Are you being sarcastic?

WILLA JO. Yep.

LIZ. You're not allowed.

WILLA JO. I'm not allowed on the roof, either.

ISAAC. Can we come up?

LIZ. Isaac—Mama said no. Listen, Willa Jo, it's not bad yet. Nobody knows about it except us. If the fire department comes, it'll be terrible, and Miss Patty will blame *me*, I know it.

WILLA JO. Why would she blame you because I'm on the roof?

LIZ. When there's fourteen people living in your house you get blamed for everything. You're my first chance to get a friend. Don't you want to be my friend?

WILLA JO. I do, more than I can say… *(Pointedly.)* But it's not up to me alone…when I come down. There are other people. Who have to agree. To come down.

ISAAC. Who?

LIZ *(gets it)*. Oh.

WILLA JO. Yes. And if we are not all in agreement, me and this other person, I have to stay on the roof.

ISAAC. Who?

LIZ. Little Sister, won't you please come down?

ISAAC. Oh!

(LITTLE SISTER shakes her head.)

PATTY *(off)*. They're not in their room.

ISAAC. Uh oh. *(Exits.)*

HOB *(off)*. They're probably in the yard, honey.

LIZ *(exiting)*. Go in the window, Willa Jo, go now!

(LIZ and ISAAC exit. PATTY enters, resolved.)

PATTY. Willa Jo—? What are those Fingerses doing in my yard?

HOB *(entering)*. Did you look in the tree—?

PATTY. They're not in the tree—they're not anywhere. You're going to have to take the car again. I can't be shouting for them like some fishwife.

HOB. What's your plan for all them rules and regulations?

PATTY. They need the rules set down. *(She waves her list.)*

HOB. They don't need a *list*—

PATTY. Goodness knows how long they've been living without clear-cut rules and regulations. Noreen was never one for enforcing the law, and that *(she looks around, then whispers)* that husband of hers, useless—absolutely without human value.

(Unseen by PATTY and HOB, WILLA JO and LITTLE SISTER listen intently to the insults.)

HOB. Patty!

PATTY. I can't help it, Hob. I'm so mad at him for running off—I'm so mad at him for making Noreen suffer.

HOB. I know. Just don't take it out on the girls.

PATTY. I wouldn't do that. I just want to give them some direction.

HOB. I agree they need direction. But they do not need a list.

PATTY. They do, they do indeed. I'm adding something to it: "You will not sneak out of the house before Aunt Patty and Uncle Hob get out of bed in the morning."

HOB. You can tell them, Patty.

(PATTY snaps her shorts. HOB takes the list.)

HOB. Let me see them rules. "All children will reply in words when they are spoken to." Why didn't I think of that? Little Sister will read that rule and start chatterin' like a beaver!

PATTY. Hob!

(ISAAC enters with dandelions.)

PATTY. What are you children doing in my yard?

ISAAC. I brought you these.

PATTY. What am I supposed to do with more—

HOB. Patty!

ISAAC. Mama said to. Flowers bring immediate calmness to the home.

PATTY. Well. Please tell your mama that…Miss Patty says thank you.

ISAAC. I got something else. I couldn't carry it all at once. *(He exits.)*

HOB. They're nice children.

PATTY. You're always taking in strays.

HOB. Patty—the lad just gave you flowers—he is nice and polite.

PATTY. His mama made him.

HOB. Well then, she is nice and polite.

PATTY. Hob. Willa Jo and Little Sister are my little sister's children, and I will be the one who makes the decisions about who they are allowed to play with. Go find them before Lucy gets here.

HOB. Those Wainwrights are as phoney as a couple of three-dollar bills.

PATTY. Cynthia is a lovely little flower—

HOB. She's a thorn bush, just like her mother. I'm going to get the car. *(He exits to the car.)*

PATTY. Hob—I am shocked beyond words at you.

(PATTY exits to the house. LIZ and ISAAC enter. They bring a plate of pie, napkins, fork.)

ISAAC. Your uncle's taking the car to look for you.

LIZ. I almost told him where you are.

WILLA JO. I'm sorry for Uncle Hob's trouble, but we're not coming down.

LIZ. My mama's going to talk to your aunt—

PATTY *(off)*. Liz Fingers—? *(Entering.)* You seen my nieces?

LIZ. Uh…

ISAAC. Here's pie!

PATTY. What?!

ISAAC. Pie!

PATTY. Why?

ISAAC. Pecan. Fresh-made last night. The last piece. It's for you from our mama.

PATTY *(brief pause)*. …Oh.

ISAAC. It's a big piece.

PATTY. I am kinda hungry—we didn't get breakfast yet.

LIZ. You mustn't start the day without breakfast.

PATTY. Yes, that's true.

LIZ. A sweet treat to start the day. Sit down here, Miss Patty.

PATTY. I don't sit on my garden gnomes. *(She sits on the steps.)*

ISAAC. Here's a napkin for your lap.

PATTY. Thank you. It's very lovely.

LIZ. It's one of our good ones.

(LIZ gives her the plate and fork. PATTY takes a bite.)

ISAAC. From our mama.

LIZ. She embroidered the design.

ISAAC. Good pie, huh?

(PATTY nods.)

ISAAC. You want milk?

(PATTY has her mouth full. Before she can protest.)

ISAAC. I'll get some. *(Exiting.)*

LIZ. Don't go—

ISAAC. I'll be right back.

LIZ. …Mama says a little sugar in the morning takes away the anger in the day.

PATTY. This is so good…why do I need anger taken away?

LIZ. Oh. Everybody needs that.

PATTY. Well…you may be right.

LIZ. It's what my mama says.

PATTY. Your mama sounds like a very…wise mama.

LIZ. I think she's wise. *(Pointedly.)* The quality she admires most is forgiveness…that you can *forgive* somebody…like when somebody makes a mistake and goes some place she's not allowed…by mistake. She should get forgiven.

PATTY. Who you talking about?

LIZ. Oh nobody! And people should be kind. She says that, too.

PATTY. Well…I agree with her. I agree with your mama.

WILLA JO. You should go meet her, Aunt Patty.

(PATTY slowly turns toward the sound. She has an internal conniption fit.)

PATTY *(enforced calm)*. Now, don't move. Don't move a muscle.

WILLA JO. How can I move? I'm cement. I'm stubborn like cement. Cement can't move.

(LITTLE SISTER approaches the edge of the roof on her butt.)

PATTY. Hold on to her— Don't move! Hob! Oh, Lord—I sent him off—

(Enter ISAAC dragging a large plant.)

ISAAC. We're out of milk— *(Sees PATTY looking at the roof.)* Uh-oh.

PATTY. If you two fall—

WILLA JO. We're not gonna. If we were gonna fall we'da done it by now.

(LITTLE SISTER sticks her foot over the edge.)

PATTY. Foot—! Foot!

WILLA JO. Little Sister, stop it.

(LITTLE SISTER stops.)

PATTY. I'm having half a heart attack.

WILLA JO *(firmly)*. We don't mean to cause you no heart attack. We didn't come up here to cause anybody a heart attack, but Baby needed…Little Sister and me… we need to be up here a while longer.

ISAAC. You already been up there all night.

PATTY. What—!

LIZ *(same time)*. Isaac—

ISAAC. Mama thought she saw them last night.

PATTY. Your mama's seen 'em, you've seen 'em—who else has seen 'em?

ISAAC. Nobody. You want us to bring some people by?

PATTY. Lord have mercy.

LIZ. Nobody can see them, Miss Patty. Mama only saw them when they stood up.

PATTY *(shock)*. Stood up? You stood up?

WILLA JO. Just I stood up. Little Sister scoots around on her butt.

PATTY. You girls, you climb back inside that window right now.

WILLA JO. Little Sister, scoot over here. *(She does.)* Don't move a muscle. Aunt Patty, we're all scooted back and we're not going to move a muscle, but…we're gonna be on the roof awhile.

PATTY. You are the most…the most…

WILLA JO. What? What am I the most of? "Useless"? "Without human value"? Just like my daddy?

PATTY. I— *(Brief pause, a defensive apology.)* Willa Jo… I never would have said those things had I known you were in earshot.

ISAAC. Can we bring over the rest of the plants? *(He points to the plant.)*

PATTY. What's that doing in my yard?

ISAAC. It's for your hedge.

PATTY. What hedge?

ISAAC. The one this plant is for.

PATTY. Hob behind this?

ISAAC. Uncle Larry.

PATTY. What's he got to do with it?

ISAAC *(frustration)*. Uncle Larry brought a truckload of hedge plants home from work. Said they're for your hedge.

PATTY. This is a very fine piece of shrubbery.

ISAAC. For your hedge!

LIZ. He can take plants home from work. They love him there.

ISAAC. The yard fairies told him you wanted a hedge.

PATTY. I sincerely doubt that.

ISAAC. They told him they need some shade.

PATTY. I *do* want a hedge. But that is not something the garden gnomes talk about.

ISAAC. You don't know what they talk about. You're in the house.

PATTY. They don't talk at all.

LIZ. You should go talk to Uncle Larry.

ISAAC. And Mama.

WILLA JO. Go on over there, Aunt Patty. You can tell her you didn't put us in harm's way.

PATTY. I'd never do that!

WILLA JO. Mrs. Fingers don't know that. She probably thinks it's all your fault. She don't know it's your out-of-control nieces.

PATTY. You—don't you move a muscle. I'm going to go inside and call Mrs. Fingers.

ISAAC. Lady.

PATTY. What?!

ISAAC. Mama's name is Lady.

LIZ. It isn't really. Everybody just calls her that because it makes her Lady Fingers. Like a little cake. Her real name is Noreen.

PATTY *(pause, already off balance, now she's toppling).* It's what?

LIZ. Noreen.

WILLA JO. Same as Mom—

ISAAC. But nobody calls her that.

LIZ. You should go on over— You can take back the plate.

ISAAC. And the fork and our good napkin.

LIZ. Yes, it might get all dirty sitting here in the yard.

ISAAC. You could thank Mama for the pie.

PATTY *(off balance)*. What?

LIZ. Only if you liked it. If you didn't like it you don't have to.

PATTY. I liked it. I liked it fine. I'm going to go thank the Lady Fingers…for the pie. *(She exits.)*

ISAAC. Bye. *(Brief pause.)* Phew! *(He sits on a gnome.)*

LIZ. You're lucky to be alive, Willa Jo.

ISAAC. Do you think your aunt will let the yard fairies visit the cave?

WILLA JO. I don't think yard fairies are allowed to visit caves.

ISAAC. Maybe they're not yard fairies.

LIZ. What else would they be?

ISAAC. Mine fairies. They're the seven mine fairies… No!!!! They're the seven dwarves. They're the seven dwarf *fairies…because (triumph)* the seven dwarves are miners!

(Enter LUCY and CYNTHIA.)

LUCY. Hello, children.

ISAAC. "Mirror mirror on the wall, who's the fairest of them all?"

LIZ. Be quiet, Isaac.

ISAAC. "Snow White is the fairest."

LUCY. Is Miss Patty here?

CYNTHIA. Who gets to be Snow White? Can I be Snow White?

ISAAC. You can be the daughter of the evil queen.

LUCY. Cynthia, be still. Are the girls here or not?

(ISAAC gestures to the roof.)

LUCY. Oh my. Hello girls. *(Brief pause.)* I thought we should get started early with your lesson. Do you need help getting down from there?

WILLA JO. No, ma'am.

LUCY. Well then, come on down.

ISAAC *(mimicking WILLA JO)*. No, ma'am.

LUCY. I'm talking to the girls on the roof, if you don't mind.

ISAAC. Where's your poison apple?

LIZ. Isaac!

LUCY. Where is your Aunt Patty?

WILLA JO. She's not here…so there can't be a lesson to-day.

CYNTHIA. My mommy don't give repeat lessons—and it's already paid for, so you better come down.

WILLA JO *(idea)*. Give our lesson to Liz.

LUCY. Lessons are nontransferable.

WILLA JO. What does that mean?

CYNTHIA. That means no.

LUCY. It means that the person who it's for has to get the lesson. And the lesson is for you and your sister.

CYNTHIA. And it's paid for, so you have to get it.

WILLA JO. We can't come down. You're going to have to give the money back.

CYNTHIA. We already spent it—

LUCY. Hush, now, Cynthia. *(To WILLA JO.)* ...Now, dear, why ever would you want to miss the lesson that your aunt wants you to have?

WILLA JO. For reasons out of my personal control, my sister and me will be unable to attend our lesson, and...unless we can work something out, Aunt Patty will need to get a refund of her money.

LUCY *(brief pause)*. Cynthia, line up those...yard figurines, we'll use them as chairs.

ISAAC. They aren't going to like it.

(LIZ starts to arrange the gnomes.)

CYNTHIA. But, Mommy—

LUCY. Just do what I say, dear.

(CYNTHIA helps arrange the gnomes.)

LUCY. Our first lesson is sitting down.

ISAAC. I can sit down already.

LUCY *(demonstrates)*. A lady selects her seat in advance of putting her *derriere* down on it, she picks out her chair, glancing at it out of the corner of her eye, approaches, stands in front of the seat, feels the seat with the back of her leg, and sits straight down. Girls, and Isaac, let's give it a try.

(As LIZ and CYNTHIA try, ISAAC plops down on the ground.)

ISAAC. This way is faster.
LIZ. Isaac. I want to learn this, okay?
ISAAC. But why?
LUCY. Because these are the secrets of the universe! While seated, a lady crosses her ankles and locks her knees firmly together.

(ISAAC locks knees and hobbles along.)

LUCY. When you rise from the chair, set your feet firmly on the ground…or the floor. Propel your body upward in a straight line. Imagine there is a string coming straight out of your head. Someone is pulling the string straight up.

(ISAAC hops himself by pulling his imaginary string.)

ISAAC. I'm a puppet, I'm a puppet.
LUCY. Now, aren't you girls sorry you missed this fine lesson?

(LITTLE SISTER shakes her head.)

WILLA JO *(same time)*. Is that the whole lesson?

(Enter HOB.)

HOB. Patty? Oh. Miss Lucy. Children. Where's my family?

CYNTHIA. Your nieces are on the roof, and we don't know where Miss Patty is.

HOB. Well, would you look at that.

LUCY. We've been having a little charm school right here in your backyard, Hob.

CYNTHIA. But your nieces stayed on the roof.

LUCY. When I give a lesson, I need my students on the ground…or…or…floor, as the case may be.

CYNTHIA. Not ten feet up.

LUCY. Not ten feet up. It was a most difficult way to give a lesson, I tell you.

HOB. But you did give it. The lesson.

LUCY. Oh, yes. I completely fulfilled my part of the bargain I have with Patty.

HOB. Then I don't see what your problem is.

ISAAC. The problem is the lesson was dumb.

LUCY. …Perhaps I had better speak with your wife. I'll be back just as soon as I take Cynthia home… Come along, dear.

(The WAINWRIGHTS exit.)

HOB. Did Patty see you up there?

LIZ *(sensing the tension)*. I guess we better go home now. Bye, Mr. Hob. Thanks, Willa Jo. And…thanks.

ISAAC. Bye, Mr. Hob.

(LIZ and ISAAC exit.)

WILLA JO. You don't understand, Uncle Hob. I know we shouldn'ta. We just had to.

HOB. Are you up on that roof to rile your Aunt Patty?

WILLA JO. No, sir, no. We needed to be up here is why. I don't mean to rile Aunt Patty. I try so hard to do what she wants. She just—she just makes me so mad!

HOB. Two peas in a pod. That's why you two rub each other so raw.

WILLA JO. No we're not—

HOB. Both older sisters. You both think you're right every time.

WILLA JO. I am right!

HOB. Yes, and your aunt thinks she's right, too.

(Enter PATTY, obscured by the plant she carries.)

PATTY. Hob? Hob. Are you there?

HOB. Yep. I found the girls.

PATTY. Give me a hand with this. *(HOB puts the plant on the ground.)* Look at that. The gnomes have been on the move again.

HOB. This is a nice plant, Patty.

PATTY. Yes, and there's about thirty more of them over there, too.

HOB. Over where?

PATTY. At the Fingerses. Larry's gonna plant them in our ditch.

HOB. Is that right?

PATTY. That's why he dug it. For my hedge. These shrubs will grow two feet a year. *(As she puts the gnomes back where she likes them to be.)* The gnomes told him they needed the shade— I'm just quoting Larry Fingers, I'm not saying I believe it.

HOB. I wondered how he found out—

PATTY. It's a different world the Fingerses live in, Hob.

HOB. I know.

PATTY. How do you know? You don't know. I'm telling you. There's so many children over there I couldn't even count them all.

HOB. Lizzie and Isaac were here, so there were only three.

PATTY. And they swarmed all over me. Like bees. One took my hand, another pulled out a chair, one brought a spoon for the coffee Lady Fingers poured me. You would have thought I was *expected.*

HOB. Expected, my.

PATTY. They sang me a song in what might have been accurate harmony, but I wouldn't know, Lady Fingers playing the piano. Then I asked her for her silence in the matter of the girls on the roof, as I didn't want her telling everybody from here to eternity about my out-of-control nieces—she said she wouldn't think of talking about the goings-on on her neighbor's roof. That would be gossip, to which she is disinclined.

HOB. You going to let Larry put in the hedge?

PATTY. No one turns down a hedge, Hob. Did you tell those girls to get off the roof?

HOB *(proudly)*. I did not.

WILLA JO. That's a nice plant, Aunt Patty.

PATTY. Don't change the subject. You coming down from there?

(LITTLE SISTER shakes her head.)

WILLA JO. ...No, ma'am. I'm sorry.

PATTY. It's no good you ma'aming me. You are misbehaving and causing strain on my health. I'm having half a heart attack even as I speak.

(LITTLE SISTER gestures.)

PATTY. What's she saying? Willa Jo, you tell me—or you are in so much trouble—

WILLA JO. She wants to know what happened to the other half of your heart.

(PATTY gasps.)

HOB. Patty—honey, she didn't mean anything by it.

WILLA JO. I didn't want to say it—you made me say it.

PATTY. I—I'm doing my best—why can't you…why can't you just…I loved Baby, too— Why don't you know that? Why doesn't anybody know that?

WILLA JO. I didn't mean—I didn't mean anything.

(PATTY and WILLA JO are in tears. HOB saves the day.)

HOB. Honey—I think we all need some *sandwiches*!

PATTY. Nobody needs sandwiches in the middle of the morning.

HOB. No, we do. I ever tell you, Patty, how I took care of my grandpa?

PATTY. Your grandpa died when you were twelve.

HOB. But I took care of him when I was seven. I didn't know what I was doing. Grandma died and Grandpa was miserable—we'd drive up there and he'd be right where we left him weeks before. My mother left me there for the whole summer figuring if he had me to take care of, he'd have to take care of himself, too.

PATTY. What was your mother thinking?

WILLA JO. Did he? Did he take care of you?

HOB. He did not. I'd have to sit next to him while he stared out the window. Pretty soon I'd be starving. So I'd make us peanut butter sandwiches. Breakfast lunch and dinner. One day he says, "I hate peanut butter." So I open up some canned ham, slice it up and put it on bread. He says, "Better, but it could use some pickles." I could make us some sandwiches, Patty.

LUCY *(off)*. Patty?

PATTY. Oh, what now? *(She tucks in her emotions.)*

LUCY *(entering)*. Patty, thank goodness you're back. *(Coldly.)* Hob.

HOB. I thought we were all done with charm for today, Miss Lucy.

PATTY. Oh, Lucy, I forgot all about the lesson. The girls aren't ready… They're…they're up there looking for cracked tiles.

LUCY. I beg your pardon?

PATTY. Tiles. Roof tiles. There's a leak. We want to find it and fix it before the rains.

LUCY. The girls are going to fix your roof?

HOB. Of course not. The girls are looking for cracked tiles. I will fix the roof. Once the girls locate the cracked tiles.

(LITTLE SISTER crawls, looking closely at the roof tiles.)

HOB. You see that? Little Sister is particularly expert in finding cracks.

WILLA JO. That's exactly why we come up here. I just forgot to mention it earlier.

LUCY. Patty, might I have a word with you? In private?

HOB. Honey, you all right?

PATTY. I'm fine, Hob. You go on in. Fix us some of them sandwiches.

(HOB goes inside through the porch door.)

PATTY. Hob, you're not…never mind—it's fine.

(LUCY gestures for PATTY to follow her out of earshot.)

LUCY. Now, Patty, I do think if we're going to have the lessons in your yard, I have to be safe, my daughter must be safe.

PATTY. What are you saying? What happened?

LUCY. The little riffraff from across the street were here when I gave the lesson.

PATTY. What did they do?

LUCY. Patty, dear. They were here, they were present. We don't know but that they have diseases.

PATTY. Why would you think that?

LUCY. When you live in filth, you have diseases.

PATTY. Their house is cleaner than mine—I was just over there.

LUCY. What on earth for?

PATTY. Pie, and…they're putting in my hedge. A new hedge all around the house. So the garden gnomes have shade.

LUCY. Who?

PATTY. The garden gnomes. They get too hot in the sun.

LUCY. Figurines do not require shade.

PATTY. Shade will do my whole house a world of good. I think you could use a little shade, too, Lucy. Maybe that's what's missing in your life. A little neighborly shade. A little ability to be kind…toward others.

LUCY. …I would never hold against you thoughtless words you spoke in haste. I would never hold it against you when your name comes up for membership in my ladies' club.

PATTY. Well. I should be sorry, of course, but you know, that may not be the kind of club I need to belong to. You know what Lady Fingers does in her spare time? She rides her brother over to the VA hospital, and while he's finishing up his treatments, she reads to the patients. I might need to belong to that kind of club.

LUCY. Darlin', you can get a rash you start fooling around with sick soldiers at the VA.

PATTY. Lady Fingers don't have a rash, and she's been going to the VA for two years.

(HOB enters onto the roof from the window. He has put on a good suit and carries sandwiches.)

HOB. Here you go, ladies. Lunch is served.

WILLA JO *(thrilled)*. Uncle Hob. You look swell.

PATTY. Hob?

LUCY. You going to fix the cracked tiles in your good suit, Hob?

HOB. Why, no. Is that how you do it at your house?

PATTY. Honey—?

HOB. Not another word, Patty. I'm going to be as careful as a man ever was. Okay?!

LUCY. No one is going to believe this.

HOB. Well, Mrs. Wainwright, maybe you better go home and call them up. Call up all them "no ones" who aren't going to believe it, and send them on over, tell them they don't want to miss the show.

(HOB begins to dance on the roof. WILLA JO and LITTLE SISTER are thrilled and happy; they dance, too.)

LUCY. Do something, Patty. Make him stop that dancing.

PATTY. This particular dance…can't *be* stopped. I believe a person must either join it, or leave the premises. How does it go, Hob? *(She attempts the dance.)* You want to dance, Miss Lucy? You can't stay unless you dance with the rest of us.

LUCY. Every single one of you, crazy crazy crazy crazy. I have no intention of refunding the money for your nieces' charm lessons. *(She exits.)*

WILLA JO. You run her off good, Aunt Patty.

PATTY. Yes, I did. And now I'm going to have to move to Venezuela.

HOB. Why we going there?

PATTY. Oh, not you, Hob. Just me. I'm going there because no one will know me. You're going to ruin that suit.

HOB. I thought I should dress up to join you girls on the roof… There's a nice view up here, Patty. I can see a lot of roofs I tiled.

PATTY. You hated that job.

HOB. I forgot how much I like being high above everything.

PATTY. You love teaching.

HOB. I do, indeed. And I also love being high above everything.

(LITTLE SISTER holds up her sandwich, gestures to WILLA JO. LITTLE SISTER wants to know the answer to the important question.)

WILLA JO. What happened with your grandpa, Uncle Hob? Did he stop being sad?

(LITTLE SISTER nods; that's what she wants to know.)

HOB. …He did not, neither one of us, but we got better. We got better because we had each other. We put pictures of Grandma everywhere— In the kitchen— In the bedrooms— Bathroom— Even the barn. Wherever we were, we had a picture of Grandma.

(LITTLE SISTER gets her painting. The girls open it.)

HOB. What's that?

(LITTLE SISTER and WILLA JO hold it open.)

HOB. Well. Would you look at that? Can you see it, Patty? *(PATTY nods, but is too moved to speak words.)* Your mom paint that?

(LITTLE SISTER nods.)

WILLA JO. Little Sister and I will get better. We have each other.

HOB. And you have me, and you have your Aunt Patty.

WILLA JO. Who does Mom have?

PATTY *(realization)*. Oh. Oh my goodness gracious…

(Enter LIZ and ISAAC carrying plants.)

LIZ. We got more plants. Is it okay?

PATTY. Of course it's okay! You bring those plants right on in here.

LIZ. Uncle Larry has a barrel full of fishhead fertilizer.

ISAAC. For your hedge.

LIZ. It really stinks.

ISAAC. It's P.U.

HOB. I can't believe Larry convinced you to take the hedge.

PATTY. Hob! Did you know this ditch was for a hedge?

HOB. Larry might have mentioned something about it.

ISAAC. Can we play with the fairies?

PATTY. Yes! I mean… Yes, you can. Sit on a gnome! Sit right down on a gnome. Make yourself at home…on a gnome.

ISAAC. We're going to need help bringing the plants.

WILLA JO *(to LITTLE SISTER)*. Do you think we can go down now? Looks like they need us down there.

PATTY. No. You stay right there. You stay right where you are. *(She goes inside through the porch door.)*

HOB. Patty?

PATTY *(from inside)*. Just stay there, Hob.

LIZ. Look, Willa Jo. I've been practicing. Watch me sit. *(She walks and sits with charm.)*

WILLA JO. I don't know why you want to be like her.

LIZ. I don't want to be like her, I just want to *walk* like her.

WILLA JO. I don't think there's going to be any more lessons.

LIZ. That's okay. There's things to practice in my magazine. We can do it together.

ISAAC. In the cave. With the seven yard dwarf miners.

LIZ. I don't think they're miners, Isaac.

ISAAC. Yes, they are.

(PATTY enters the roof from the window bringing a phone with a long cord.)

PATTY. Take this, Hob.

HOB. Honey—! ...Welcome to the roof.

PATTY. Hold the phone— No, hold me. Hold me, Hob, help me, Hob.

HOB. Girls, make room. Don't look down, honey.

PATTY *(dials)*. Just hold tight to my belt loop.

ISAAC. Is she calling the fire department?

LIZ. I don't think so.

PATTY. Hi, Noreen, it's me. How you feeling, sweetie?... Good, that's really good...because we need you to take a ride on over here. I'm on the roof, and you'll never guess who's with me. Willa Jo, and Little Sister, and Hob, too. And we're not going to come down... No, we are not coming down until you get here. So drive carefully, but don't dawdle because I'm scared to death, and the girls need to pee... Great. I love you. *(Hangs up.)* Okay, your mom's on her way. She's going to rescue us from our roof emergency.

(LITTLE SISTER stands up and crosses her legs.)

PATTY. Oh, you really do have to pee, don't you?

(LITTLE SISTER nods.)

PATTY. Come here.

(LITTLE SISTER sits in PATTY's lap.)

PATTY. I'll hold you…and you hold the pee. Okay?

(LITTLE SISTER nods.)

PATTY. Come here, Hob, Willa Jo.

(WILLA JO and HOB tuck in on either side of PATTY and LITTLE SISTER. The FINGERSES look on. PATTY speaks to WILLA JO.)

PATTY. What were you two thinking? Why ever did you come out on the roof anyway?

(The briefest of pauses as WILLA thinks how to explain.)

LITTLE SISTER. We were getting near to Baby.
WILLA JO *(brief pause)*. We were getting near to Baby.
PATTY. Well. *(Brief pause.)* That's fine. That's just fine.

(They hold on.)

THE END